The
Secrets
of
Coral Reefs

CROWDED KINGDOM OF THE BIZARRE AND THE BEAUTIFUL

BY DWIGHT HOLING

ONDON TOWN PRESS

The London Town *Wild Life* Series
Series Editor
Vicki León

The Secrets of Coral Reefs
Principal photographer
Howard Hall

Additional photographers
Frank Balthis; Tom Bean; Jay Carroll; Dorothy Cutter; Helmut
Horn; Chris Newbert; Doug Perrine; Lindsay Pratt; Ed
Robinson; Carl Roessler; Geoffrey Semorile; Marty
Snyderman; Norbert Wu

London Town Press
P.O. Box 585
Montrose, California 91021
www.LondonTownPress.com

Book design by Christy Hale
10   9   8   7   6   5   4   3   2   1

Printed in Singapore

Distributed by Publishers Group West

Publisher's Cataloging-in-Publication Data
Holing, Dwight.
The secrets of coral reefs : crowded kingdom of the bizarre
and the beautiful / Dwight Holing ; photographs by Howard
Hall [et al.] —2nd ed.
p. cm. — (London Town wild life series)
Originally published: San Luis Obispo, CA : Blake Books
©1993.
Summary: Explores the creation, growth and life of coral
reefs, examining the rich plant and animal species that live
within these warm water ecosystems.
Includes bibliographic references and index.
ISBN 0-9766134-3-3
1. Coral reefs and islands—Juvenile literature. 2. Coral reef
ecology—Juvenile literature. 3. Coral reef animals—Juvenile
literature. [1. Coral reefs and islands. 2. Coral reef ecology.
3. Coral reef animals.] I. Hall, Howard. II. Title. III. Series.
QH541.5 H863 2005
595.789—dc22
2005930188

FRONT COVER: On a Red Sea reef, a pair of clown anemonefishes
—protected by a mucous coat—happily hang out among the
anemones. The female fish even lays her eggs near the deadly,
stinging tentacles. To repay their host, these little Nemos chase
away anemone nibblers, like butterflyfish.

TITLE PAGE: At 700 pounds or more, the tridacna clam is a
whopper. Its blue "lips" are actually the fleshy mantle of the
clam. Inside it are tiny helpful plants called zooxanthellae that
make food for this giant.

BACK COVER: Tourists watch the sun set over Truk lagoon in the
South Pacific. Gentler tourism is just one of the actions needed
to save incredible ecosystems like the coral reefs at Truk.

BACK COVER INSET: Coral reef animals adapt to their environment. A forcepsfish on a Hawaiian reef has a long snout that
lets it eat without getting stuck by urchin spines. A false eye
spot near its yellow tail helps fool predators.

Contents

A *vast world underwater*

Although we call it "earth," we live on a water planet, blue with ocean over two-thirds its surface. Among the ocean's wonders lies the biggest structure ever built by living creatures: the Great Barrier Reef. Stretching more than 1,250 miles off the coast of Australia and transforming into a towering underwater skyscraper in places, the reef is comprised entirely of coral. This rich ecosystem, along with thousands of other massive hard-coral reefs around the globe, was

◄The South Pacific islands of Palau have it all: atolls plus barrier and fringing reefs. Over 300 species of hard corals and 1,300 species of reef fishes live here. Palau's reefs are threatened by coral bleaching and by rainforest logging, which smothers corals with muddy runoff.

constructed by an animal as soft and small as a pencil eraser.

Meet the coral polyp, nature's master builder. By partnering with a primitive plant, this simple animal has created an underwater paradise as colorful and complex as the tropical rainforest on land.

You'd never peg a polyp as a grand builder—or a meat-eater. But it's both. At night, it extends wee tentacles, looking like a miniature flower. As microscopic animals float by, the polyp's flowery tentacles snag them.

To keep from being eaten, early in life the polyp builds a hard chalky cup around itself. It gets help from a type of algae called zooxanthellae. One square inch of coral may hold several million of these algae.

Zooxanthellae are wizards at chemistry. Like other plants, they use sunlight to make sugar. They also recycle the wastes of their host into more nutrients. From the algae, the lucky coral polyp gets 80 percent of its food. But it does its share, too. Each night, the food caught by the polyp provides the one thing algae cannot make: nitrogen for both of them.

What else does the zooxanthellae get out of the deal? A place to live and access to light, its main requirement. Even underwater, algae need sunshine. That's why all 794 species of reef-building corals live in oceans that are clear and shallow—so that sunlight can reach their plant partners. During its lifetime, the polyp soldiers away, adding material to its hard cup. As it grows,

▼ During the day, the coral polyp hides in its hard fortress. This is how Acropora, the most common variety of hard coral, looks when the polyp is in hiding.

▼ At night, each polyp of the Acropora hard coral ventures outside its hard skeleton. Waving delicate and sticky tentacles, it catches plankton and other floating particles.

it connects itself to other polyps to form colonies. When it dies, the polyp leaves behind its white skeleton of calcium carbonate, a material almost identical to our own bones.

Over time, millions of skeletons compress into limestone, forming the reef itself. Reef building is a slow process. Eventually, linked colonies of coral can stretch for hundreds of miles underwater. Only the top layer of reef contains live polyps that are still busy, building.

Although coral is hard, seastars find it delicious. Butterflyfish, filefish, and parrotfish also munch and crunch it, turning

coral skeletons into sand. Worms, mollusks, and others burrow into the reef, leaving it as holey as Swiss cheese.

With all these coral eaters chipping away, you would think that a coral reef would eventually collapse like a house full of termites. Fortunately, another plant called coralline algae comes to the coral reef's rescue. It also produces calcium carbonate—but behaves like cement. In its crusty form, it grows over hard coral, filling in holes and making the reef strong. On some reefs, such as those in the Northwestern Hawaiian Islands, coralline algae covers more area than coral itself. Coralline also forms tough algal ridges on top of reefs. This keeps the reef from being eaten away by big waves.

▼ The crown-of-thorns seastar is a coral-eating nightmare. Once, its numbers were kept in check by predators like the triton shell. But collectors have removed many live tritons from the reefs. This may be why the hungry seastar is a menace.

▼ Hydrozoan coral is often called fire coral for the tiny harpoons or nematocysts it carries. In spite of its looks, it's closer to a jellyfish than a coral polyp.

Hard coral species come in many shapes and sizes. Some climb upward, like pillar and blind man's cane. Other treelike species are staghorn, fastest growing coral in Australian waters, and elkhorn, the speed demon of the Caribbean. A number of species make round formations, as brain and star corals do. Still others grow in hard sheets or plates. They get names like lily pad, lettuce, vase, and sea fan.

Hard coral family members have distinctive shapes, and usually appear in softer shades of green, blue, violet, cream, brown, and yellow.

Not all corals are hard or stony. Another type of fast-growing polyp produces soft corals. Their colonies can contain thousands of individuals. Instead of reefs of stone, these jelly-skinned beauties look like bizarre plants or trees, with see-through trunks, inflatable branches, and starbursts of color. On their branches, they wear spiky bits of calcium, called spicules.

◄ Hard coral species, like this white plate coral with purple fringe, race to grow over other corals. The overhangs made by corals provide new shelter for animals like the cobalt seastar, with its rubbery blue arms. On the dome of a brain coral rests a yellow-lip banded sea snake. To hunt, this very toxic character can hold its breath for two hours.

For extra defense, soft corals produce toxins that make them taste bad. Like the hard corals, many species have helpful zooxanthellae inside their bodies.

Soft corals often form underwater gardens, blooming in fingerpaint shades of fiery red, hot pink, flaming orange, royal purple, and knock-your-eye-out golds. Certain species are bright blue.

Corals get some of their color from zooxanthellae inside them. But many species—such as the zippy orange popcorn coral—carry their own pigments, too. Some pigments act as sunblock, protecting both algae and polyp. Different colors permit coral to live at different depths.

There are other coral species that live without plant partners, like the willowy gorgonian. Some corals live alone, not in colonies. One species of psychedelic-looking, pink and purple mushroom coral grows ten inches across—and all of it is one humongous polyp!

A more recent discovery are the cold-water corals, living in deep waters, sometimes on underwater peaks. They don't need sunlight yet act like trees, adding layers, year after year, to their hard exteriors. These corals amaze biologists; some are over 8,000 years old, and extend for nine miles underwater.

Learning who's who and what's what on a coral reef isn't easy. Plants and animals grow over, under, inside, and on top of each other. Telling the plants from the animals is just as hard.

Reef-building corals thrive in two places: the Caribbean region, including the Gulf of Mexico and the Atlantic; and the much larger Indo-Pacific region, which includes the Pacific and Indian oceans.

Biologists who study coral reefs sort them into three main categories: fringing, barrier, and atoll.

Fringing reefs are the youngest and the most numerous. They are found close to shore—on the fringe of land. The reef facing the land side typically rises out of the water.

Barrier reefs are more mature structures, bigger than all others in size and grandeur. Australia's Great Barrier Reef holds the world record for size. Next biggest? The barrier reef off Belize in Central America, followed by the Florida Keys.

Thanks to their location, barrier reefs act as buffers, or barriers, between land and sea. These unsung coral heroes protect coastlines and the human beings on them from wave action, hurricanes, and other weather extremes.

The third reef type, called an atoll, forms when a volcanic island collapses and slides beneath the sea. As the coral reef expands, it makes a circle of small low islands around the calm waters of the lagoon that is left.

Often found in mid-ocean, atolls come

▶ **Soft corals may look like fantastic plants but they are colonies of tiny animals. They grow up, down, or sideways, often clinging to the wall of the fore-reef. In the fight for space, soft corals and sponges use toxins. Clams and seastars squeeze in somehow.**

◄ Star coral is a heavyweight among reef builders. A hard coral, it often grows in boulder shape. On a crowded reef, the star coral adapts. It forms flat green plates, in this case around a colony of sponges.

in all sizes. The Indo-Pacific alone has over 300. If you felt like building 15,000 Egyptian-style pyramids, you could do it with the coral from just one average atoll! The world's largest is Kwajalein, whose atoll surrounds a lagoon of water 60 miles across. Atolls can be ancient. Near the equator, atolls 50 million years old have been found in the Marshall Islands.

Although a few cold-water reefs can be found off North America and Europe, the vast majority of coral reefs are located between the Tropic of Cancer and the Tropic of Capricorn, a 3,000-mile-wide band that circles the world around the equator.

Hard-coral polyps can't perform their magic in just any old sea. They need a solid base to settle on, and warm, shallow water—about 75 degrees Fahrenheit—but no hotter. They require saltwater that's free of mud, sand, slime, and excessive plant life. That's why corals can't get a foothold off the coasts of Brazil, India, or West Africa. The mighty rivers in those regions flush too much mud into the ocean.

Soft corals grow deeper than hard corals can. Other species like spiral wire coral survive at 100 feet or more below surface. Made of protein rather than calcium carbonate, its black coral skeletons are now rare.

From fossil remains, scientists know that coral polyps were once widespread. That changed when continents began to drift and the seas rose and fell. About 9,000 years ago, the Indo-Pacific region took over as the center of development for modern coral reefs. Meanwhile, on the other side of the world, other kinds of polyps became confined to the Caribbean Sea.

That's why coral reef systems are so different today. The rich Indo-Pacific region hosts 92 percent of all reefs. These reefs have ten times the number of hard coral species as the Caribbean. Only eight types of hard coral grow in both areas; the most common is star coral. As for fishes, there are six times as many species on Indo-Pacific reefs than on Caribbean reefs. An almost unspoiled Indo-Pacific system, like the Northwestern Hawaiian Island Coral Reef Ecosystem Reserve, can have over 7,000 marine species.

No matter where they grow, all coral reefs offer biological riches. A quarter of all sea species either live in these ecosystems or depend on them for food.

Coral reefs around the planet are also subject to the same threats to their existence: global warming, invasive species, human disturbance, overfishing, and pollution, to name a few.

Soft corals look bushy and plump,
often wearing lipstick reds and pinks.
Schools of fairy basslet fishes flash
and spin above this coral garden.
Reef builders, like the tree coral at
left, often wear quieter colors. At
night, hard corals dress up. The
polyps inside emerge from the stony
skeletons to feed, making the coral
look like a flower.

A crowded kingdom

Like tropical rainforests on land, coral reefs are warm, wet, bursting with life forms, and three-dimensional. Because they grow horizontally, diagonally, and vertically, reefs offer niches, nurseries, hunting grounds, and hiding places aplenty. Each area of the coral reef receives different amounts of sunshine and shade, temperature and current.

At the reef crest, where wave action is hardest, live the creatures that know how to hang on: red coralline algae, barnacles, and low-growing or sturdy corals.

The oceanside zone is called the fore-reef. Its shallow upper layers are jagged, with spurs of reef that jut outside, and channels that go deep inside. Big corals live here. Eels and fishes have their choice of crevices. Large predators, from sharks to barracudas and tuna, patrol this food-rich hunting ground.

Below this area, the fore-reef becomes a wall painted with colors, on which corals fight for space and sunlight. The stately pillar, a hard coral, feeds in daylight hours. So do soft corals. Other hard corals wait until twilight to put forth their feeding tentacles.

As the fore-reef goes deeper, hard corals disappear and soft corals thrive, competing for space with rainbows of sponges, anemones, sea fans, and seastars. Although they appear locked into place, many of these creatures, from soft corals to anemones to seastars, can move. Time-lapse photography has shown us their travel secrets.

One slow wanderer is the crinoid. This filter feeding dancer clings to the wall, waving hundreds of Technicolor arms to catch tidbits floating by. If its perch fails to please, it can crawl or swim to a better one.

Smaller creatures decorate every reef surface, and riddle it with hidey-holes.

◀ In clear Caribbean waters, bat stars and algae can easily be seen by snorkelers. Sea urchins graze on green algae plants in a delicate balancing act. Too much algae can smother the reef. Too many urchins can hurt it, too.

Christmas tree worms open like pop-up books, extending tinsel-colored gills so that larvae stick to them like holiday ornaments.

At night, nudibranchs stalk the reef, chugging along in one unhurried meal. As they hunt, these tiny snails without shells wear gorgeous velvety ruffles and plumes, filled with nasty stingers from hydroids they've eaten.

▼ Bright colors on the reef can mean, "this critter stings" or "tastes bad." The nudibranch, a type of snail without a shell, is able to borrow weapons by eating the stinging cells of hydroids—picking up their poisons somehow without getting a stomachache.

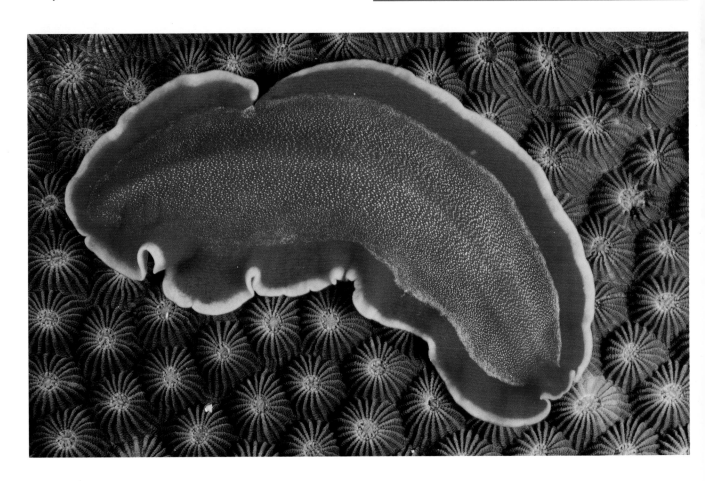

Shelled critters, from mollusks to bivalves, graze on thick mats of turf algae. For shelter, some dig into the reef. These nooks and crannies later become dens for many species of scavengers, like crabs and lobsters. To avoid trouble, the decorator crab holds an umbrella of live sponges over its back, or puts stinging hydroids on its antennae. The boxer crab puts live anemones on each of its

▶ Dancing, tousle-headed crinoids bring movement and drama to the reef wall. Related to the seastar, these filter feeders wave five to 200 feathery arms to nab their microscopic meals.

◀ Most human beings will never touch a giant eel, or get to see a coral reef in person. But all of us can love the reef from afar, by respecting and protecting its wonders.

▲ Even though it has big teeth and thick scales, the parrotfish is hunted by moray eels and sharks. Some parrotfishes spin see-through sleeping bags to mask their scents from predators each night.

claws—the hermit crab plunks one on its shell.

Moray eels reign as kings of the crevices. Some species behave as ferociously as they look. The viper moray uses its curved, six-inch-long jaws to pluck unfortunate fishes that pass by like a ghoulish jack-in-the-box. Not so the pink and yellow snorkel-nosed moray. Comic and friendly as its name, it will pose for underwater photographers.

Another zone of abundant life lies near the protected back side of the reef: the sandy bottom and calm waters of the lagoon. Here, among turtle grass meadows, octopuses stalk, flounders lurk under sand for smaller prey, and dolphins look for hidden fish—like flounders. Turtles cycle through the lagoon, hunting lobsters. Sometimes they find easy pickings. Each fall, spiny lobsters on Caribbean reefs migrate to mate, walking single file across the bottom.

Venomous sea snakes go for air at the surface, then travel to the sandy bottom to hunt. These critters can hold their breath up to two hours. Their long, skinny relatives, the garden eels, often rest in the sand like a group of oversized exclamation marks.

Because they move constantly, and are so plentiful, fishes make the reef come alive. Most aren't shy retiring types. Reef species often dress to kill, flaunt body designs like tattoos, and sport combat-ready spikes, fins, and mouth parts. They have names as colorful as they look: chocolate hind, lemon meringue angelfish, lined sweetlips, shy toby, bloody bigeye, Red Sea raccoon butterflyfish. Many species are as slender as compact discs. When they turn sideways, they do a disappearing act.

Fluorescent angelfishes, winking on and off, dart crazily. Schools of fairy basslets flicker through the clear water. An Achilles tang uses a big orange polka-dot to point to its sharp weapons. Surgeonfish hover, looking like pancakes smeared with butter and dripping with blueberries.

Like their namesakes, parrotfishes have powerful beaks and glow in iridescent greens, blues, and other colors. With molars in their throats, they grind up coral in order to get to algae, their primary food. Many a tropical beach owes its sand to the parrotfish, which can grind five tons of rock into sand each year—per fish!

▲ Wrasse fishes go head to head in a dispute over territory. Male fishes make open-mouth gestures and puff up their bodies to win females and scare rivals.

There isn't much elbow room on a coral reef, even if you have fins instead of elbows.

To survive, animals and plants rely on defense mechanisms, feeding strategies, and mating rituals. They also compete and cooperate in an extraordinary number of ways.

Plankton, the ocean's nomads, are plentiful. Some are microscopic plants called phytoplankton. Others are zooplankton, tiny animals like copepods or crab larvae. They are eagerly eaten by large and small, from whale sharks to coral polyps. Although it seldom helps them survive, most plankton are transparent—making them invisible.

Schooling, where hundreds or thousands of fishes swim in unison, is a common behavior. Fishes do it for extra speed, taking advantage of less water resistance behind fellow fishes. They also school to fool predators. Distracted by the movement of so many swimmers, a hungry shark or ravenous turtle often misses.

By schooling, fishes find mates, search for food more effectively—and sometimes muscle in on new territory. Convict surgeonfishes team up to invade the algae fields defended by lavendar tangs.

Territory provides a ready source of food and shelter, so many species stake their claims. Some, like mottled blennies, become very attached to their digs.

Many fish species are scrappers. A tiny damselfish will blitz a trespasser no matter what size. The blueline surgeonfish patrols its territory by swimming around its

▼ On the reef, partnerships are common. Inside a living brain coral, the blenny fish finds a snug hole, left by a Christmas tree worm. The brain coral gets its shamrock color from tiny plants inside it, called zooxanthellae. Both coral and plants supply nutrients to each other.

◄ Coral reef partners sometimes play two against one. A homeless shrimp may team up with a meat-eating anemone. To earn its keep, the shrimp pretends to offer cleaning services by wiggling its antennae at passing fishes. Fish that get within stinging range of the anemone find themselves getting cleaned for dinner! The shrimp gets the scraps.

boundaries. When another fish comes close, the blueline swims alongside, a big hint for the intruder to move along.

Because living quarters are tight, many coral residents make alliances with neighbors. Mutualism, or partnerships that are helpful to both parties, are found throughout the natural world. Coral reefs abound with them.

Thanks to the film "Finding Nemo," the best-known odd couple on the reef is the clown anemonefish and the anemone. Most fishes avoid the deadly stinging anemones. But this five-inch daredevil lives, nests, and hides among its tentacles. Biologists think that each little Nemo is protected by a mucus-covered coat.

To return the favor, the clown anemonefish, like a watchdog, chases away the handful of species that like to eat its host, making a barking noise as it does so. The anemone also shares quarters with helping algae, our old friends zooxanthellae.

In the Indian Ocean, the long-spined hatpin urchin lets smaller neighbors like the clingfish and the shrimpfish live among its needles. An ominous, glorious pink creature called the cauliflower jellyfish does the same for a tiny fish called the silver medusa, living amongst its tentacles.

In the West Indies, some species of sponges and shrimps become partners. Wring out a single loggerhead sponge, and out will fall 16,000 shrimp. These sponges are so big that two human divers could squat inside of one. Many of the 5,000 species of sponges provide homes for a multitude of creatures, from mollusks to fishes.

Other two-way partnerships involve grooming. With one gulp, the tiger grouper could devour a hundred gobies, but it doesn't. Instead, the big lunk opens its cavernous mouth and allows gobies to tidy up. The cleaners dine free, on all the leftovers, parasites, and dead tissue they can eat.

Dozens of species of fishes, crab, and shrimp set up permanent cleaning stations for their services. During rush hour on the reef, fishes often wait in line to be groomed!

Commensalism, where only one party benefits, is another sort of partnership. Sharks and manta rays don't seem like the types to share. Often, however, they let remoras hitchhike as they circle the reef. Remora fishes have suction-cup mouths, sticking tighter than Velcro to the bodies of these

▼ A grouper opens its mouth for a wrasse to enter and start scrubbing. Some 30 species of fishes, crabs, and shrimps operate reef cleaning stations. As the photo shows, many wear stripes to advertise. Fishes sometimes wait in line to get a going-over. The cleaners swim away with a free meal: parasites, dead tissue, and leftovers.

▼ When a crinoid stops feeding, it closes its arms, as the curled arms with white showing on top have done. Crinoids often position themselves on sponges or algae of a contrasting color.

▲ Seastars like this cobalt blue aren't speedy. Sometimes they escape predators by leaving a limb behind. This painless tactic, called autotomy, lets the animal grow a new arm—or even two. Crabs and lobsters can do this as well.

► At night, crinoids crawl or swim to a good spot for filter feeding. As they sway gently in the current, they appear to be on tiptoe.

▲ Snazzy in blue and gold, the triggerfish is fifteen inches of bad temper. Its sharp teeth do a number on clam shells. The triggerfish also can blast jets of water, knocking over urchins and uncovering crabs.

Threespot damselfish are farmers, growing crops of algae. While they never have to worry about droughts, damselfish must battle urchins that can mow down an algae field, if given a chance. The clever three-spot carefully picks up the urchin with its teeth, hauls it away—then dumps it onto someone else's turf.

The urchin, a voracious feeder on algae and kelp, has another arch-enemy—the triggerfish. This handsome blue and gold fish has teeth that can crack a clamshell. It can also blow jets of water. The trigger-fish uses its firehose spray to blast an urchin, knocking it over. While the spiky urchin is up-ended, the triggerfish makes a meal out of its unprotected underside.

Hunting season is open all year on coral reefs, so camouflage is always in style. Quick-change artists like the flounder melt into sand and other backgrounds by mimicking the surface they are near. In one experiment, a flounder was able to match the pattern of a checkerboard! (After that feat, let's hope he got the day off.)

Octopuses offer more colorful action than an internet pop-up ad. In less than a second, an octopus can go from thick to thin, alter its skin texture, turn from red to white–and keep on doing it.

Most reef fishes wear markings that hide them or mimic their surroundings. When the redband yellowtail hovers in a forest of sea whips, it becomes just another whip. Turning pale, it develops two black stripes the length of its body. Several species of butterflyfish wear false eyespots on their tail ends to puzzle predators.

An old pro at ambush, the frogfish changes

huge animals, feeding on food scraps but giving back no known benefit to their hosts.

Peaceful coexistence is wonderful, but all creatures great and small still need to eat. Some fishes graze, others farm. Most hunt. Angelfishes cruise over the surface, targeting mollusks, algae, and worms. Butterflyfishes have fine, hairlike teeth that make short work of tubeworms. Wrasses have hinged jaws that open wide for thick-shelled prey. Sponge for dinner doesn't sound very nutritious, but it is filling for puffers, Moorish idol fishes, turtles, and cowry shells.

► Sea urchins wear weapons on their top sides, but underneath they are soft and defenseless, as this upside-down urchin shows. The triggerfish knows the secret of flipping an urchin for a quick meal. The urchin has a mouth—the star-shaped organ in the center—but it can't bite back. It's a plant grazer.

its color and spots to blend with nearby sponges. On its nose, it wears a piece of flesh shaped like a fishing pole. As it hunkers down, the frogfish bobs its built-in lure to tempt the curious. Few can resist the bait.

A skinny relative of the seahorse, the trumpetfish plays a different deadly tune. As it hangs from a sea fan or finger sponge, it mimics them. When an unwary fish passes by, bingo! breakfast. At times, this cunning hunter straddles a passing parrotfish for cover, using it to get closer to its prey.

Even though coral polyps don't move as adults, they have ways to compete for space.

Fast growing corals do it by overtopping, hoarding the life-giving sunlight to themselves and leaving their rivals in the shade.

Slower growers directly attack their competitors. The star coral, one of the few reef-builders to live in both the Caribbean

▼ Flatworms and bristleworms are small carnivores that hunt on gorgonian, a non-building coral that looks like a fan.

► Filled with more empty space than solid flesh, the sponge is the reef's most ancient animal. It's been around for some 600 million years.

and the Indo-Pacific regions, grows in the shape of a boulder or a plate. When it feels cramped for space, it goes vertical—and gets aggressive. Opening a hole in its own body, it squirts digestive juice that eats away its neighbor.

Other coral species use thin filaments to reach over and digest the tissue of a coral that's come too close.

Soft corals play rough also. By releasing toxins into the water, they kill or discourage nearby hard and soft corals.

Although sponges often cooperate with other species, they know how to give their predators a nasty shock. Scientists are deeply interested in the chemistry of sponges. The chemicals they use to rid themselves of bacteria, fungi, and hungry sponge-eaters are varied and valuable.

► Inside the hollow bodies of sponges live thousands of fishes, shrimps, crabs, feather duster worms, and nudibranchs. Surprising sponges can mimic algae, or grow big as a barn. Found everywhere, sponges are especially magnificent on coral reefs.

▼ The cowfish lives on the barrier reef in Belize. In the dappled light of the reef, its bold markings provide camouflage for the fish.

Besides the next meal, mating is the big priority for coral reef dwellers. Most species reproduce in huge numbers. They have to, because their eggs and young are small, defenseless, and tasty to other species.

Many reef species, from fishes to invertebrates to coral itself, get their cues to spawn from the moon, the length of the day, and other environmental factors.

The black clownfish breeds on a strict lunar schedule. Twice a month, females lay between 200 to 400 eggs. The hatchlings emerge during the full or the new moon, when waters are at their highest and swiftest. The tides carry planktonic larvae, perfect food for the clownfish newborns.

Gobyfishes are a twosome. A goby couple digs an elaborate burrow on the seafloor, where the female lays her eggs. When she exits, the male takes over. To make sure he does his job, the female seals him inside the burrow. Four days later, she lets him out so they can tend the young together.

► Sponges might lack brains and heart but they have timing. They often spawn as a group, all at once. When they do, clouds of eggs and sperm curl upwards, like smoke. Later, sponge larvae will float away to find a new spot to settle.

◄ Over 100 species of coral polyps spawn at the same time. This is a brain coral in action; its eggs and sperm will soon form huge clouds underwater. In time, the few coral larvae that survive will make new coral colonies far away.

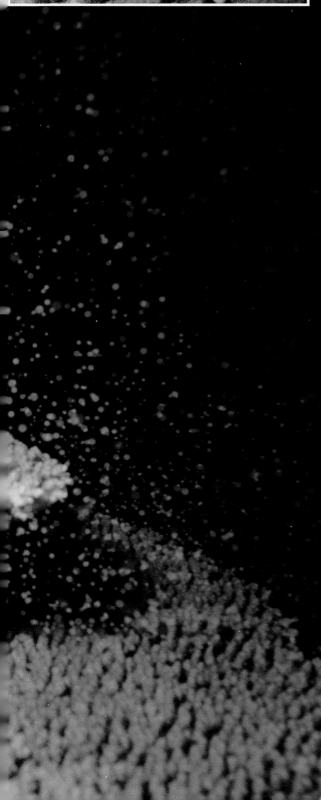

Saddle-back butterflyfishes bond so tightly that one will stop feeding and look for its mate if they become separated. When they reunite, male and female celebrate with a ritual, swimming around each other at close range for a few minutes.

Other species, like the bluehead wrasse, the lyre-tail coralfish, and some hamlets, tend to mate in groups. Female fishes of the clown wrasse even live in groups called harems; so do whitetailed humbugs.

Sponges often breed together and all at once. In late August, entire communities of male and females coordinate to produce a collective release of sperm and eggs.

◄ Like a slow-motion fireworks display, coral reefs explode underwater in community spawnings. Triggered by cues from the moon and sun, these magical mass matings occur yearly in the Coral Sea, on the Great Barrier Reef, and elsewhere. Other reef animals, such as sponges, also spawn all at once.

◀ A bristleworm is a bite-sized beauty that few want to tackle. One fiery, hairy mouthful, and would-be predators learn to leave these noxious rainbows alone.

This steamy display resembles clouds floating through the water. Divers in the Caribbean call them "smoking sponges."

Coral colonies have varied strategies. Some slow-growing species do not breed yearly. Coral species in the Red Sea spawn in different months. In the Gulf of Mexico, the brain and star corals in the Flower Garden Banks national marine sanctuary spawn together each August.

In contrast, when it's spring on Australia's Great Barrier Reef, over 25 percent of all the coral species fire their reproductive hopes. This huge underwater explosion, first seen in 1982, looks like a fireworks display. It's so big that there are enough eggs and sperm to feed many hungry predators, and enough left for a new generation of corals as well.

Coral polyps also reproduce asexually. They are able to bud, or clone themselves, from a large parent polyp. Their close relatives, the anemones, do the same thing.

Most amazingly, three-fourths of hard coral colonies, and many other coral reef inhabitants, are individually both male and female. This hermaphroditism—the ability to change genders at will—solves the problem of finding the right mate for slow-moving polyps.

Similarly, in the Caribbean, the harlequin bass reaches maturity with two sets of reproductive organs and can perform as a male or a female, depending on who it meets. The wrasse fish goes about it differently. It starts out as one gender and changes into the other. So does the clown anemonefish, which begins life as a male. Once grown, the largest anemonefish metamorphosizes or changes into the dominant female. And the second largest fish? It gets to play the dominant male role.

Reef animals also use sound underwater to compete, meet, and mate. Hundreds of fish species make vocalizations. In his algae garden, a bicolor damselfish male cranks his swim bladder to make chirping sounds, a sure-fire lure for females. If another male shows up, the damselfish makes a "get lost!" pop. To chase away other males, grouper fishes slam their gill covers to make a booming sound.

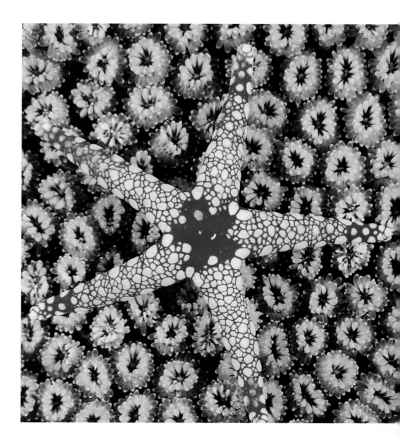

▲ Millions of seastars brighten coral reefs around the world with candy-cane colors and outlandish patterns. Slow but tenacious, a seastar opens shellfish with its tube feet, then ejects its stomach over prey to digest it.

At times, the coral reef resounds with sound effects from cownose rays, oyster toadfishes, roughneck grunts, and many other species—including the warbles of reef visitors like humpback whales. Even though colors shift underwater, reef animals from fishes to cephalopods use body coloration to communicate.

Distinct colors and different markings show the species, sex, status, availability, and age of a given fish. When fishes change gender, or go from juvenile to adult, they also change wardrobes. Blue tangs, parrotfishes, and countless other species change color and patterns three times in life.

Creatures looked at as prey by many reef animals use color to blend in. For a fish, that might mean spots and hues that resemble its favorite patch of corals. For a worm or a shrimp, it might mean matching the Day-Glo yellow or the shocking pink of a sponge called home.

Bright colors also play a big part in the mating game. On the crowded reef, bold markings allow species to find one another and carry out courtship. Once squid have paired off, the two of them glow and blush as they swim in circuits.

Color, and the ability to change it, also works as a threat. Many fish species turn brighter colors as they fight rivals. Color warns, it welcomes, it camouflages, it tricks, it lures—and coral reef dwellers know how to read all its messages.

Reefs in the balance

▲ People used to think this clam could trap divers with its huge shell. But the giant tridacna is a harmless bivalve. Its meat feeds many communities. Once threatened by overfishing, the tridacna is now farmed on South Pacific islands.

Given the abundance of coral reef plants and animals, and their reproductive activity, you'd think that reefs would never be endangered. Sad to say, coral reefs have plenty of enemies.

Some enemies are part of nature. Typhoons, hurricanes, and tsunamis can wreck reefs. Storms topple coral and destroy newly hatched young. Too much rain can make reef waters less salty. River currents and volcanic activity can smother corals in mud or dirty water.

At times, plant and animal populations get out of balance. Although several kinds of algae are vital to the reef, too much can kill it. Or take the crown-of-thorns seastar. It craves quantities of coral. Just one can devour a huge area of polyps in a day. Periodically, this pest kills off miles of reef. The triton trumpet is about the only predator of the crown-of-thorns seastar. The triton is also a favorite with shell collectors. When the living population of tritons drops sharply from human collectors, the crown-of-thorns becomes a plague.

Directly or indirectly, human activities

► Millions of people now own tropical fishes and live corals. To stock seawater aquariums, divers often use poisonous cyanide to stun fishes. This kills many fishes and part of the coral reef too.

put reefs in peril. Reefs have become a big destination for tourism. But reefs are often brutalized by boat traffic, plastic debris, and careless practices while diving or swimming.

Equally deadly is the world's growing appetite for tropical fishes, corals, turtles, seahorses, and exotic shells. Although a few species are raised for sale, most are wild caught and exported from reef-rich places like Indonesia.

Collecting methods are gruesome. Blast fishermen use dynamite to tear coral apart and stun reef fishes. Divers pour cynanide in crevices to capture specimens. Repeated use often poisons the whole reef.

For millennia, people everywhere have lived off the food bounty of the reef. But overfishing and wasteful practices have taken a horrible toll.

As a result, marine fisheries for many species of fish and shellfish are in collapse everywhere.

Activities on land have deadly consequences on the reef. Developers mine coral and pulverize reefs to build roads and harbors. Logging tropical rainforests and mangrove trees fills

► Coral reefs from Bali to Florida still look beautiful and untroubled. But huge problems threaten their survival. Pollution and global warming are reef killers. So is overfishing and the over-harvesting of live seashells, pictured here.

nearshore ocean waters with silt—a leading cause of reef damage in the Philippines and elsewhere.

Ocean pollution can be felt up and down the food web of the coral reef. Sewage contaminates shellfish; spilled oil suffocates coral polyps. Chemical wastes poison filter feeders.

As if these factors weren't enough, reefs have another powerful enemy: coral bleaching. When seawater gets too warm, coral polyps get stressed. They expel their helpful algae and turn ghostly white; if the condition continues, colonies die.

First noted in 1983 in the Caribbean, bleaching events have hit harder and wider since then. Major reefs from Belize to Australia have experienced serious bleaching. One out of five reefs may already be lost—and many scientists predict that 60 percent of the world's reefs will vanish in our lifetimes. The link between global warming, coral bleaching, and reef death becomes ever clearer.

Like other warning signs in the natural world around us, coral reefs are trying to tell us something about the fate of our oceans and our beautiful blue planet.

Saving our coral kingdoms

▶ Reefs sometimes form circular lagoons called blue holes. This one in Belize, Central America, is a favorite of divers. Other blue holes are found in the Bahamas and around Australia.

A coral reef is one of nature's greatest accomplishments—and one of humankind's benefactors. Its polyps remove carbon dioxide from the atmosphere. Its reefs protect our shorelines from storms and erosion. This ecosystem feeds millions of us, and acts as nursery for new generations of fishes and invertebrates. But a reef has limits to what it can withstand.

Reefs ended up where they are, because conditions were just right. They cannot adapt. The creatures of the coral world have no options, either. They cannot take up new homes, like the hermit crab. The gutsy clown anemonefish, the glorious soft corals, the hard-working algae and polyp partners—all must live on the reef, or die without it.

What do coral reefs need to survive and thrive?

More worldwide protection, more laws, more teeth in existing laws. More people of action, young and old, as watchdogs for the reefs. More attention paid to the value

of intact coral reefs and mangroves, the shock absorbers that saved countless lives in the tsunami disaster of 2004.

More attention paid to bigger things, like global warming—the major cause of climate change, warmer ocean waters, and coral bleaching.

More attention paid to smaller things: gentler tourism, less development in areas where coral reefs grow. More shells and corals left on the reef, instead of on coffeetables or imprisoned in home aquariums.

What can you do to save the coral kingdoms? Educate yourself and others. Get involved in groups like Reefwatch and Rescue the Reef Project. Help scientists to gather data that will protect and heal reefs, through organizations like Earthwatch. Join reef cleanups, from the Florida Keys to southeast Asia.

On this water planet, water connects us all. You don't have to get near a coral reef, to kill one. You don't need to see a reef, to love one. The fate of the reefs is our destiny too.

Coral reef secrets

- At 700 pounds, the tridacna clam is the heavyweight mollusk of the reef.

- Seashells from the reef can be deadly as well as pretty. All 500 species of coneshell use their noses as fleshy harpoons to deliver poison.

- The Great Barrier Reef—world's biggest—runs nearly 1,300 miles along the coast of Australia and can be seen from space.

- Loggerhead sponges are huge and empty enough to hold 16,000 shrimp—or two human divers.

- To hide from eels and sharks, the parrotfish uses mucus! At night, the parrotfish rests inside its slimy "sleeping bag."

- Popcorn coral is bright orange, and its pigment acts as sunblock.

- One atoll reef has enough coral in it to build 15,000 pyramids.

- Some reef fishes have startling abilities. The blue tang changes colors three times. Others change from male to female.

- The size of a pea, the coral polyp could not build reefs without the help of its tiny plant friend: an algae called zooxanthellae.

- Coral reefs can be noisy places. Shrimp sound like pistols, damselfish chirp, barnacles click, and groupers boom, using their gill covers.

◄ Soft corals don't have stony skeletons, like hard corals do. Inside their fleshy bodies, they carry small pieces of calcium to make them stiffer. Most soft corals grow in colonies but do not build reefs.

Glossary

Atoll. A coral reef growing around a shallow body of water called a lagoon. Most atolls are far from land.

Autotomy. The ability of animals like seastars and octopuses to lose a limb painlessly, then grow a new one.

Barrier reef. The most common type of coral reef. It usually grows along a coastline, acting as a buffer between land and sea.

Bleaching. The result of stress on coral polyps because of too-warm water or other environmental reasons. They eject their algae helpers, become white and often die. Global warming may cause coral bleaching.

Commensalism. A relationship between two species where one provides help, but is itself neither helped nor harmed. A type of symbiosis. Compare to mutualism.

Coralline algae. A pinkish-red algae plant that acts as cement for coral reefs, making them stronger.

Ecosystem. The physical environment of a coral reef, a stable community of plants and animals where nature is in balance.

Fore-reef. The part of a coral reef that faces the ocean. On a mature reef, it may form a wall that descends for hundreds of feet.

Fringing reef. A coral reef attached to land.

Harem. The name given to a group of females in some fish species, gathered by a male in order to fertilize their eggs.

Hermaphroditism. The condition of having both male and female reproductive organs within one body. Certain coral reef fishes, sponges, and other animals and plants have this quality.

Lagoon. A body of calm shallow water, found inside an atoll or between the reef crest and the shoreline.

Mutualism. The cooperative behavior between certain animals and other animals or plants, common in a reef, such as where one fish "cleans" the teeth of another fish and so gets a meal. A type of symbiosis. Compare to commensalism.

Nematocysts. Stinging cells used by anemones, jellyfish, and coral polyps to catch prey.

Nudibranch. A family of brightly colored small snails without shells. They are able to eat nematocysts without harm and become poisonous themselves.

Photosynthesis. The process that allows plants like algae to convert sunlight into food, like sugars.

Plankton. Microscopic ocean wanderers which are a key food source for many reef creatures. Phytoplankton are tiny floating plants. Zooplankton are tiny animals or larvae.

Predator. An animal that hunts other animals for its food.

Prey. An animal that is hunted.

Reef crest. The highest part of a coral reef, where the wave action is strongest.

School. A group of animals, usually fishes, that swim together for safety and other reasons.

Symbiosis. A close, long-lasting relationship between animals or plants of two different species that usually benefits them both.

Zooxanthellae. Plant algae living inside coral polyps that provide most of their food. Without these helpers, most hard and soft corals could not live. Anemones, sponges, and clams also benefit from zooxanthellae partners.

About the author

California writer **Dwight Holing** has authored books on natural history, the environment, and eco-travel.

Photographers

Fourteen outstanding wildlife photographers contributed unusual imagery to this book. Principal photographer was Howard Hall. Front cover of Red Sea reefs by Chris Newbert; back cover of Truk Lagoon by Geoffrey Semorile; forcepsfish inset by Ed Robinson. Frank Balthis, p. 39; Tom Bean/DRK Photo, p. 16; Jay Carroll, pp 6 left & right; Dorothy Cutter, pp 7, 11, 27 bottom; Howard Hall, pp 8-9, 19, 20, 27 middle, 27 top, 38, 40-41; Helmut Horn, pp 34-35, 35 inset; Chris Newbert, front cover; Doug Perrine/DRK Photo, p. 33; Lindsay Pratt, pp 12, 29 top, 36, 30 inset; Ed Robinson/Hawaiian Watercolors, pp 14-15, 18, 37, back cover inset; Carl Roessler, pp 1, 4-5, 7 left, 30-31; Geoffrey Semorile, pp 28, 32, back cover; Marty Snyderman, pp 21, 22, 26, 29 bottom, 42-43; Norbert Wu, pp 23, 24-25

Special thanks

- Michele Roest, Outreach & Education Specialist, Monterey Bay National Marine Sanctuary
- Julie Dahlen, children's services librarian
- Joni Hunt, special research
- Jay Carroll, marine biologist
- Tenera Environmental
- Robert "Troutman" Allen, Jr.
- Howard Hall, cinematographer
- Helmut Horn, nature photographer

Where to see coral reefs

- Visit aquariums, zoos, and parks with coral reef exhibits. Note: to preserve wild corals, some aquaria use manufactured reefs. Places in the U.S. with outstanding coral exhibits include: Seattle Aquarium, WA; Aquarium of the Pacific, Long Beach, CA; Shedd Aquarium, Chicago IL; Columbus Aquarium, OH; Aquarium for Wildlife Conservation, NY; National Aquarium, Baltimore MD; Audubon Aquarium of the Americas, New Orleans, LA. Waikiki Aquarium in Honolulu HI has the foremost collection of living corals. Its conservation efforts include growing 2,600 pieces of coral for other aquaria. www.waquarium.mic.hawaii.edu/coral. A partial list, outside the U.S.: Coral World Ocean Park on St. Thomas, Virgin Islands; Parque Oceanique Cousteau, in Paris France; the Antilles Underwater Park and Aquarium in Curacao; and ReefHQ Aquarium in Townsville, Australia. ReefHQ Aquarium is the world's largest coral reef aquarium, offering 130 coral species, 120 fish species, and behind-the-scenes tours. For further ideas, browse the worldwide directory at www.coralreef.org/directory
- Visit real coral reefs. Magnificent examples from Florida to Fiji, Australia to the Antilles, Hawaii to Mexico. When choosing lodging, dive guides, and tour companies, look for eco-friendly companies and sustainable tourism that benefits local people. Two standouts: the Coral Reef Classroom at Florida Keys National Marine Sanctuary: PO Box 500368, Marathon FL 33050; www.fknms.nos.noaa.gov; and Glover's Reef Marine Research

Station in Belize: www.wcsgloversreef.org. Also visit websites of the helping groups listed elsewhere on these pages.
- Armchair travel through coral reefs via DVDs, videos, and books. See our recommended list on these pages.
- Take a hands-on part in scientific projects on coral reefs. A great place to start is Earthwatch Institute, connecting volunteers with scientists and critical field research on coral reefs and other projects worldwide for 30 years. Teacher programs, scholarships, opportunities for kids 16 and up—and their parents. 3 Clock Tower Place, Suite 100, Box 75, Maynard MA 01754-0075. www.earthwatch.org

Helping organizations and good websites

- The National Marine Sanctuary system, www.sanctuaries.noaa.gov, protects 14 areas—nearly half with coral holdings--from the Florida Keys to American Samoa, including the nearly pristine Northwestern Hawaiian Island Coral Reef Ecosystem Reserve.
- Another informative website related to NOAA – the National Oceanic and Atmospheric Administration – is the Coral Reef Information System (CoRIS) at http://coris.noaa.gov.
- A portal at http://coralreefreport.info has a rich list of links to many worthy websites, including marine sanctuaries and reserves by name and a dozen photo-filled sites.
- International Coral Reef Information Network (ICRIN) and its partner, International Coral Reef Action Network (ICRAN), offer masses of clear, current data. Outstanding resources for students and teachers; photobanks, databases, fact sheets, and links aplenty. www.coralreef.org and www.reefbase.org
- Reef Relief, PO Box 430, Key West FL 33041, an active local organization which has done much to reverse damage, protect

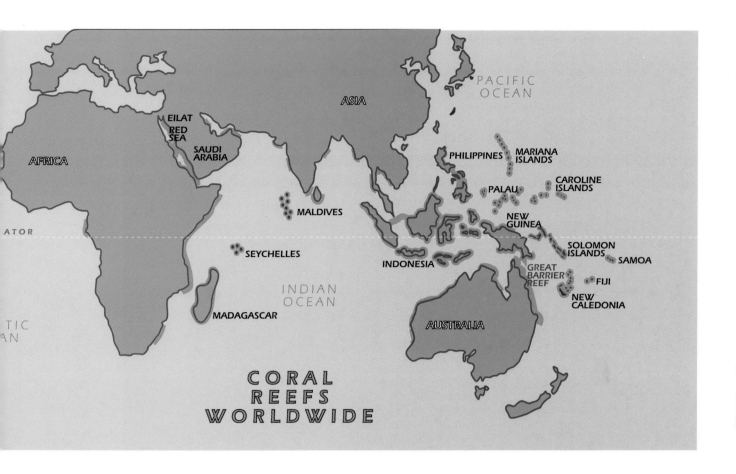

CORAL
REEFS
WORLDWIDE

coral ecosystems in the Florida Keys, and link up with other programs in the Bahamas, Cuba, Honduras, and Jamaica. Their kid-friendly website says, "If you're not outraged, you're not paying attention." www.reefrelief.org.

- From Australia, the Great Barrier Reef Marine Park Authority and the University of Queensland offer accessible, well-linked sites at www.gbrma.gov.au and www.reefedu.au.

Space doesn't permit details of all worthy sites on coral reefs. Try this outstanding handful:

- Monterey Bay Aquarium, www.mbayaq.org, offers easy to read fact sheets by species, with conservation notes.
- Coral Reef Alliance promotes conservation, gentle tourism, advice to divers at www.coral.org
- Jean-Michel Cousteau's www.oceanfutures.org
- Discovery Channel's entry at www.discoverychannel.com includes sound effects of coral reef inhabitants.
- www.marinebio.org, gives useful, detailed info by species.
- www.biosbcc.net/ocean has clear text and photos on the coral polyp.
- www.wcs.org sponsored by the New York-based Wildlife Conservation Society, details their programs in Kenya, Asia, and Belize.

To learn more
Books
- *World Atlas of Coral Reefs,* by Spalding, et al. (University of California Press 2001). Huge book, accessible text for motivated readers. Excellent maps, aerial photographs, and photos from space (underwater pictures can be small).
- *Are the World's Coral Reefs Threatened?* By Charlene Ferguson. (Greenhaven Press 2004). Good book for YA readers.

- *Reef Life: Natural History & Behaviors of Marine Fishes & Invertebrates,* by Denise Tackett, et al. (Microcosm Ltd 2002).
- *Coral Reef, a City That Never Sleeps,* by Mary Cerullo. (Cobblehill Books 1996) and *Coral Reef,* by April Sayles (Twenty-First Century Books 1996): older but well written and still valuable.

Videos & DVDs
- "Coral Reef Adventure." Macgillivray Freeman Films Educational Foundation. 2004 2-disc DVD and IMAX film. 42 minutes. In this stirring footage above and underwater, filmmakers Howard and Michele Hall capture the most beautiful and threatened reefs in the world.
- "Island of the Sharks." Howard Hall Productions/NOVA/WGBH Boston. 2002 DVD and IMAX film. Shot by the superb filmmaking duo of Howard and Michele Hall at Cocos Island off Costa Rica, the footage is as much on coral reefs as on the sharks that inhabit it. Unusual animal behaviors and sights.
- "Jewels of the Caribbean Sea." National Geographic 1994 VHS format. 60 minutes. Stunning visuals, again captured by cinematographer Howard Hall.

Other A-V educational materials
- "Jean-Michel Cousteau's World, volume 1: Cities Under the Sea Coral Reefs." Interactive CD, photos with animation, convey the wonders of this ecosystem. www.oceanfutures.org/Nemo.
- "Coral Kingdom." CD and resource guide. Four units with multimedia slide show and computer research activities. Details at www.cyberlearn.com/coral.
- "Dive Back in Time," other short films, slide sets on DVD, plus an updated 2004 *Coral Reef Teacher's Guide.* www.reefrelief.org

Index

Photographs are numbered in **boldface** and follow the print references after **PP** (photo page).